WIP 23
by Frances Bukovsky

All works included within this document are property of Frances Bukovsky. Contact the author for sales of individual pieces or further inquiry of work at flbukovsky@gmail.com or www.francesbukovsky.com. This work was first produced in 2019.

Our lives are incomplete stories, works in progress composed of more moments than we seem to remember.

Between these pages are moments that have fallen between the cracks, landscapes frozen in imperfect emulsions, the forgotten spaces where my thoughts have lingered over the past year.

Incomplete thoughts

and idle daydreams.

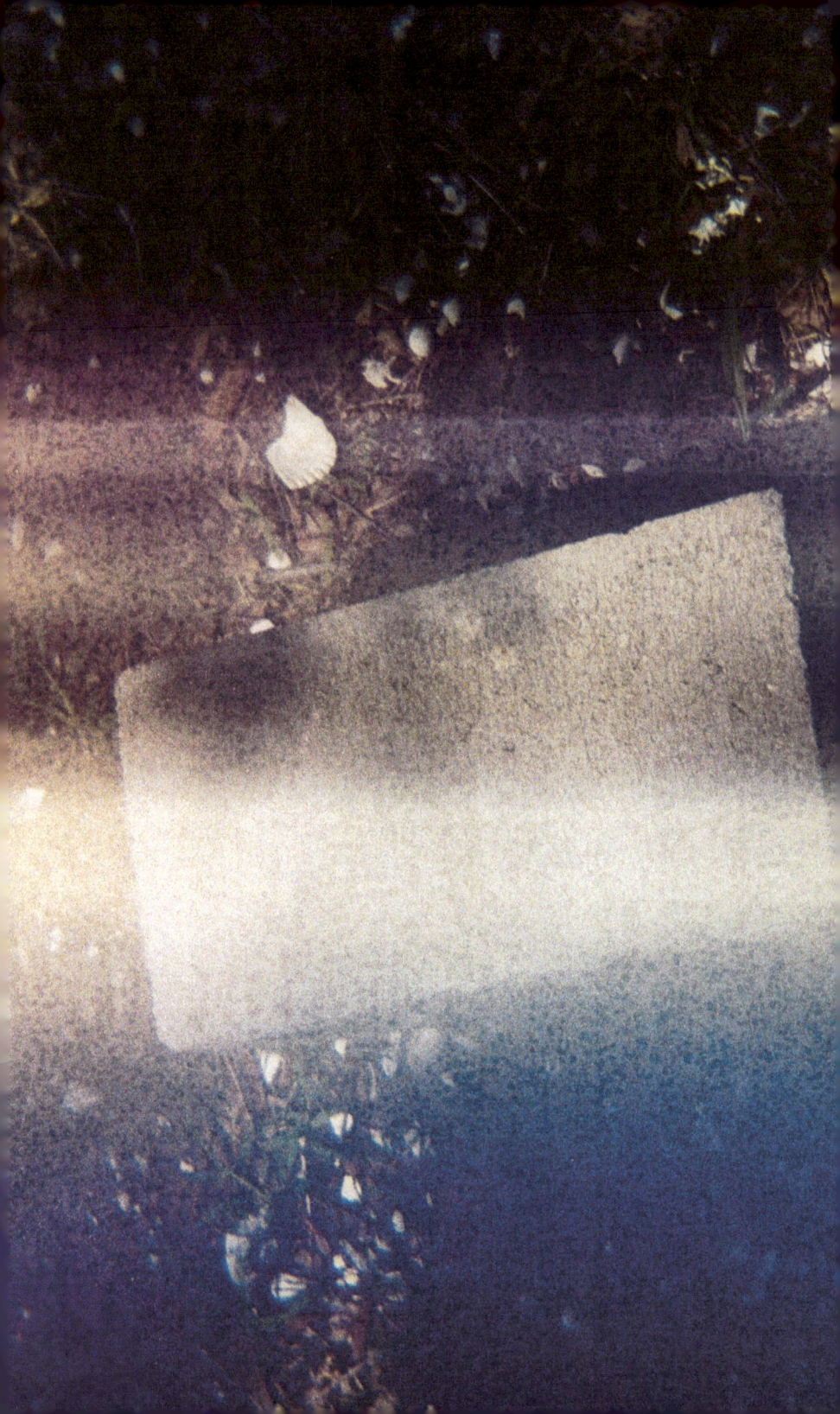

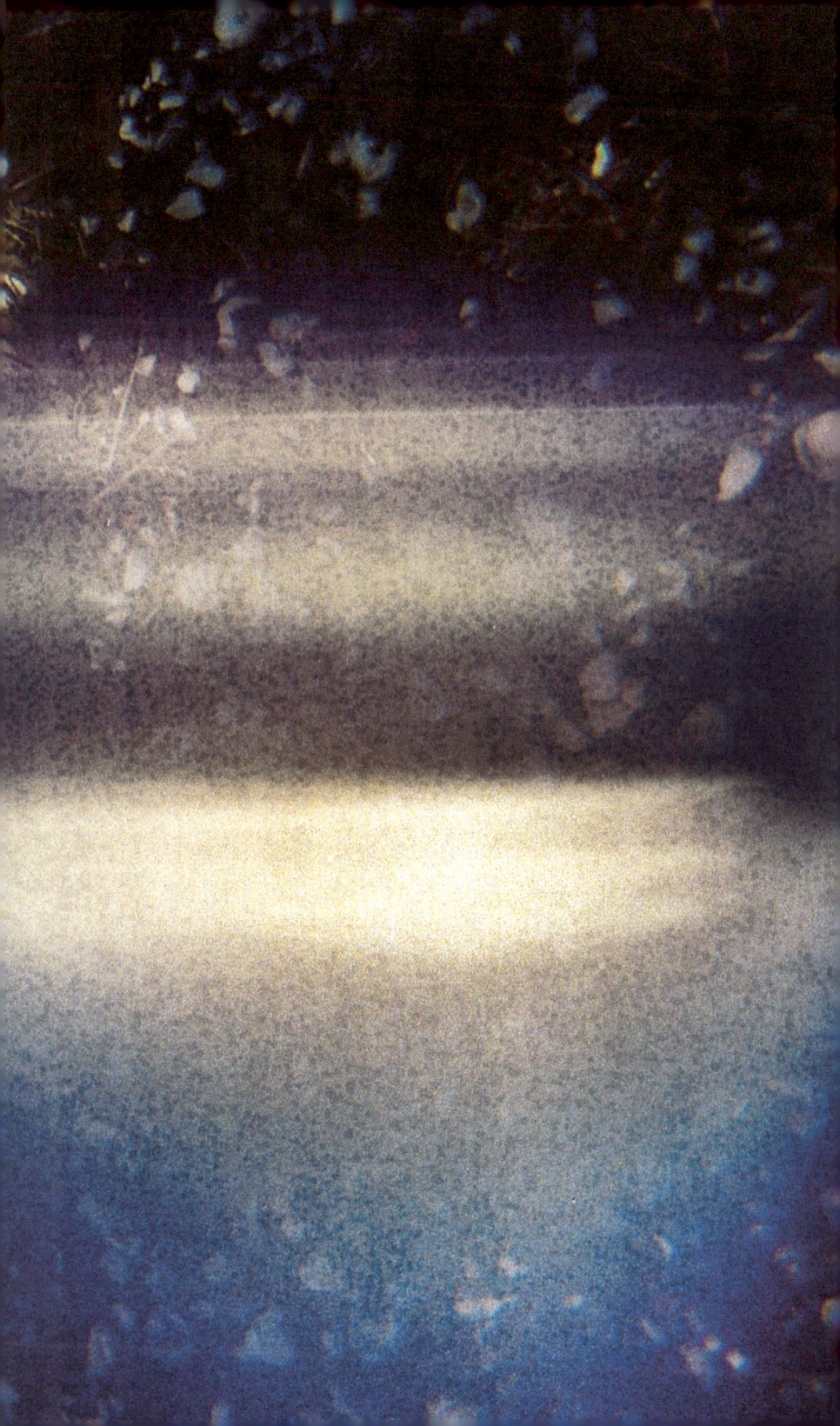

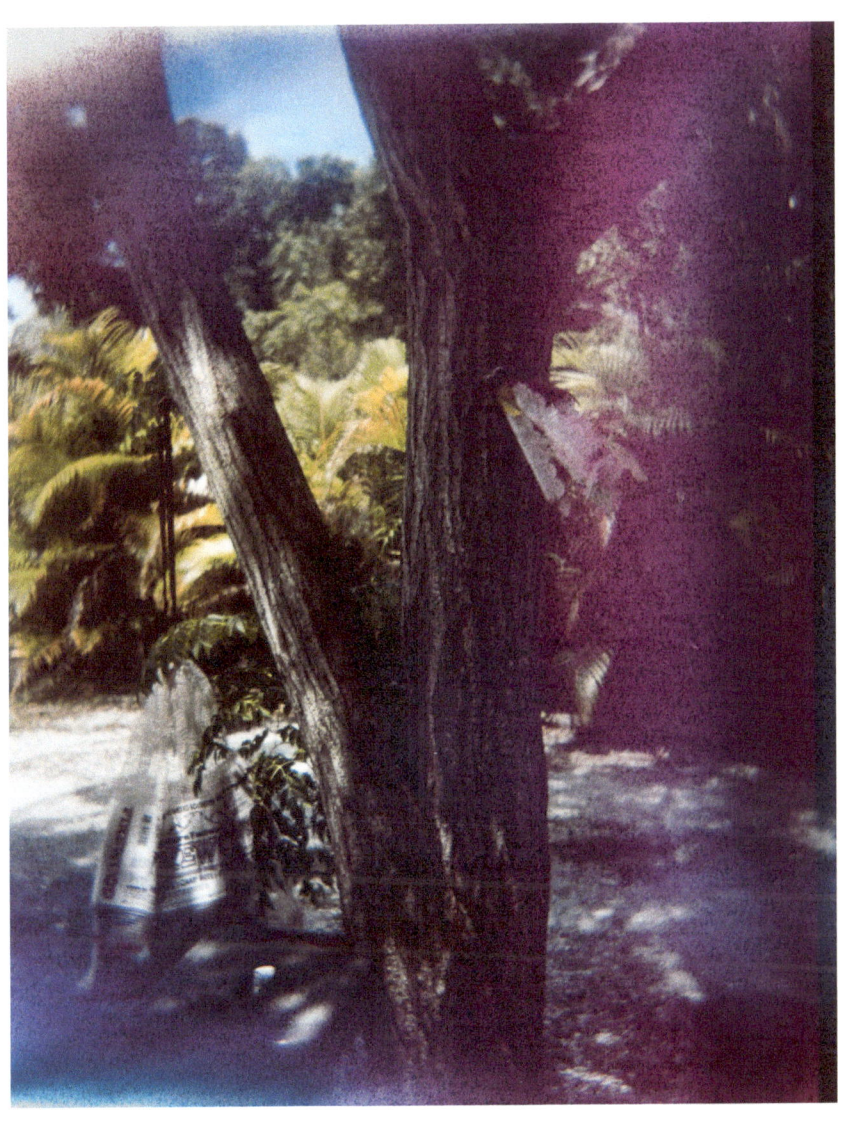

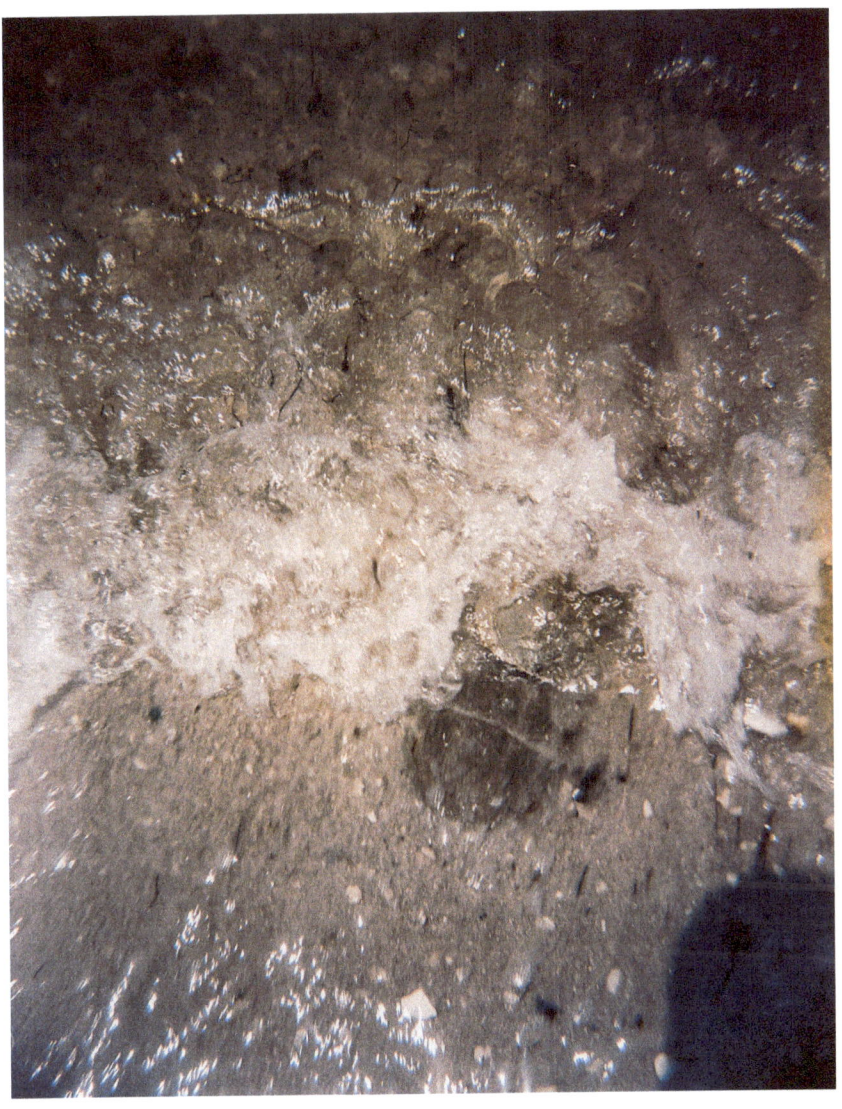

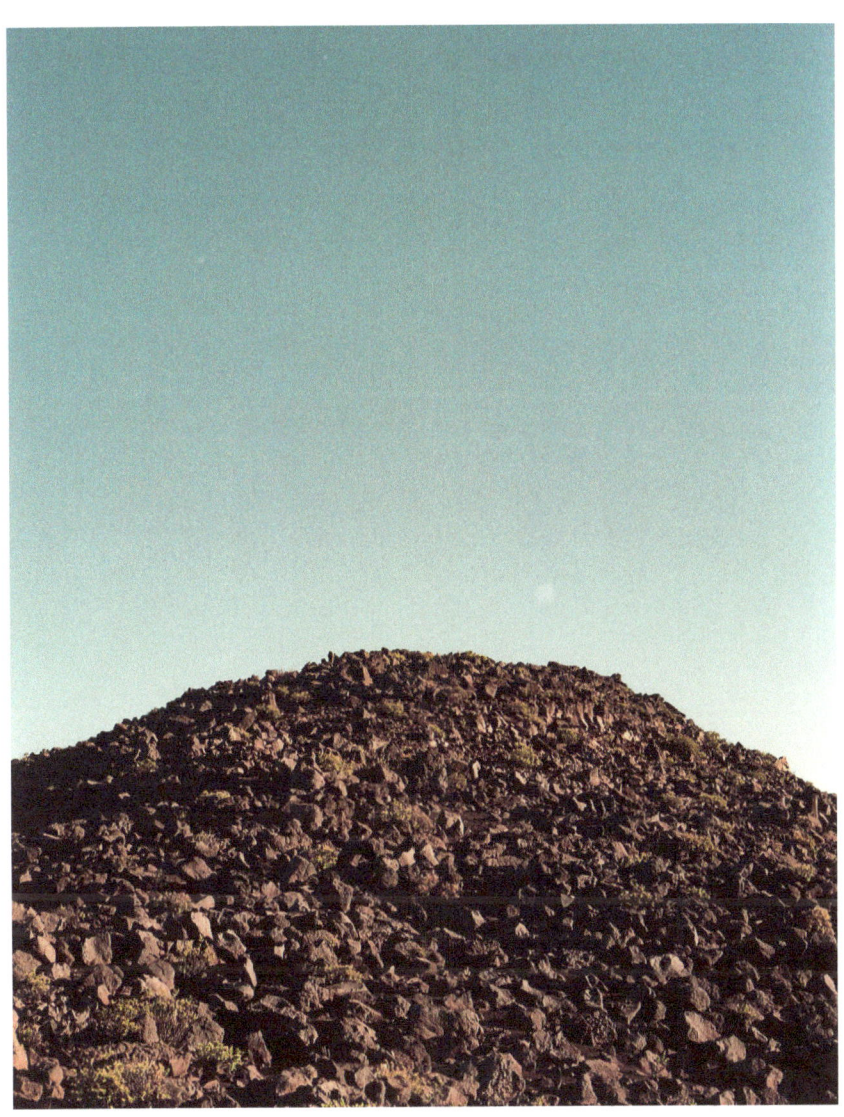

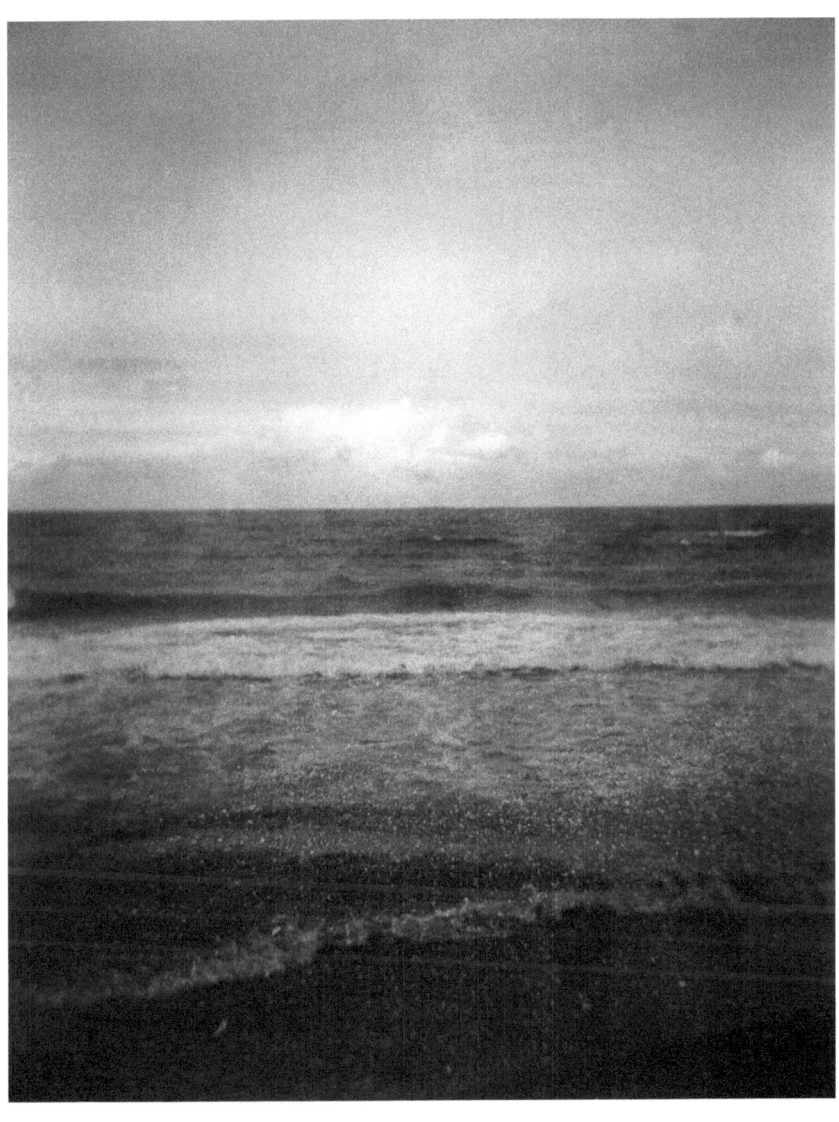

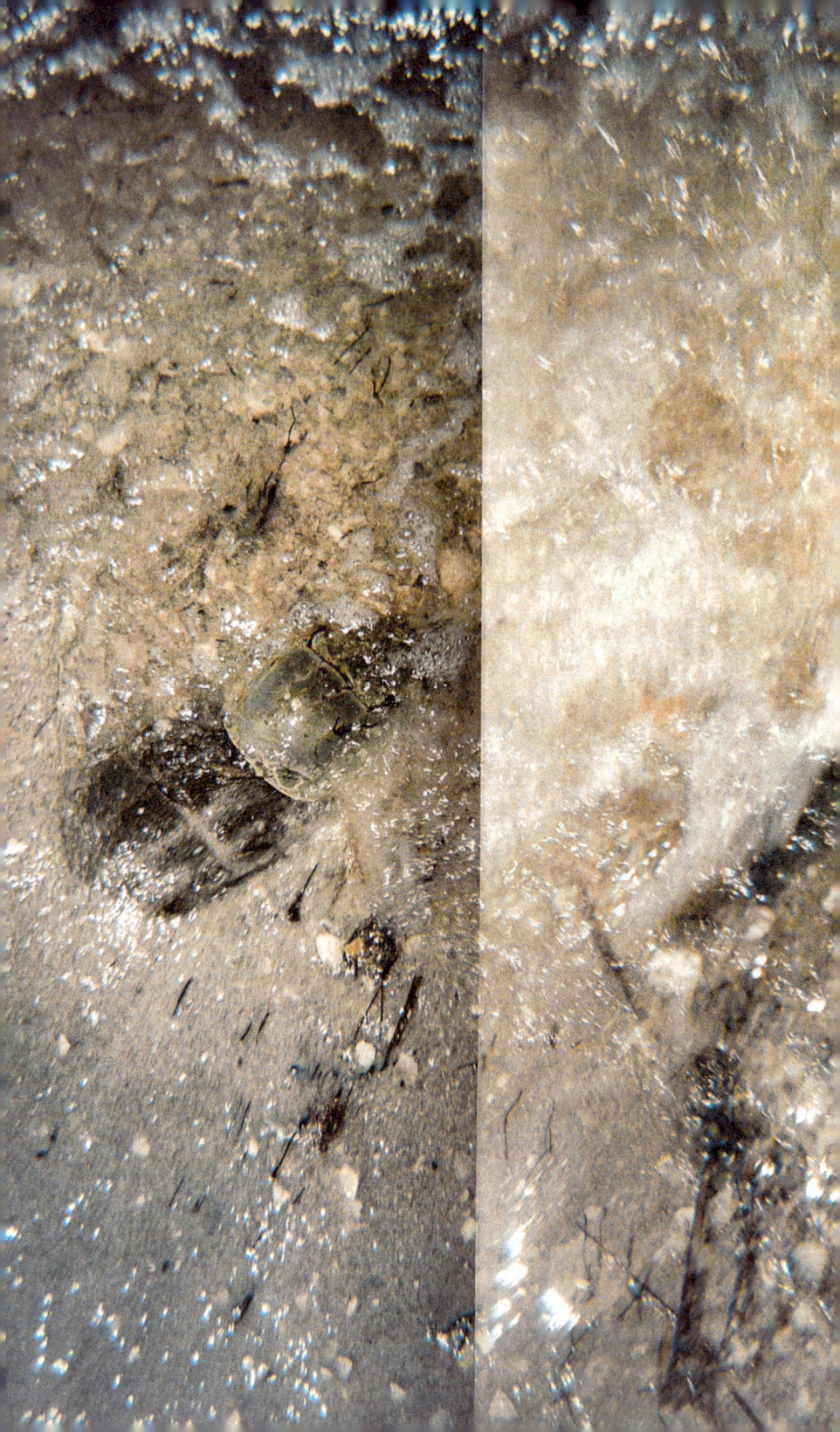

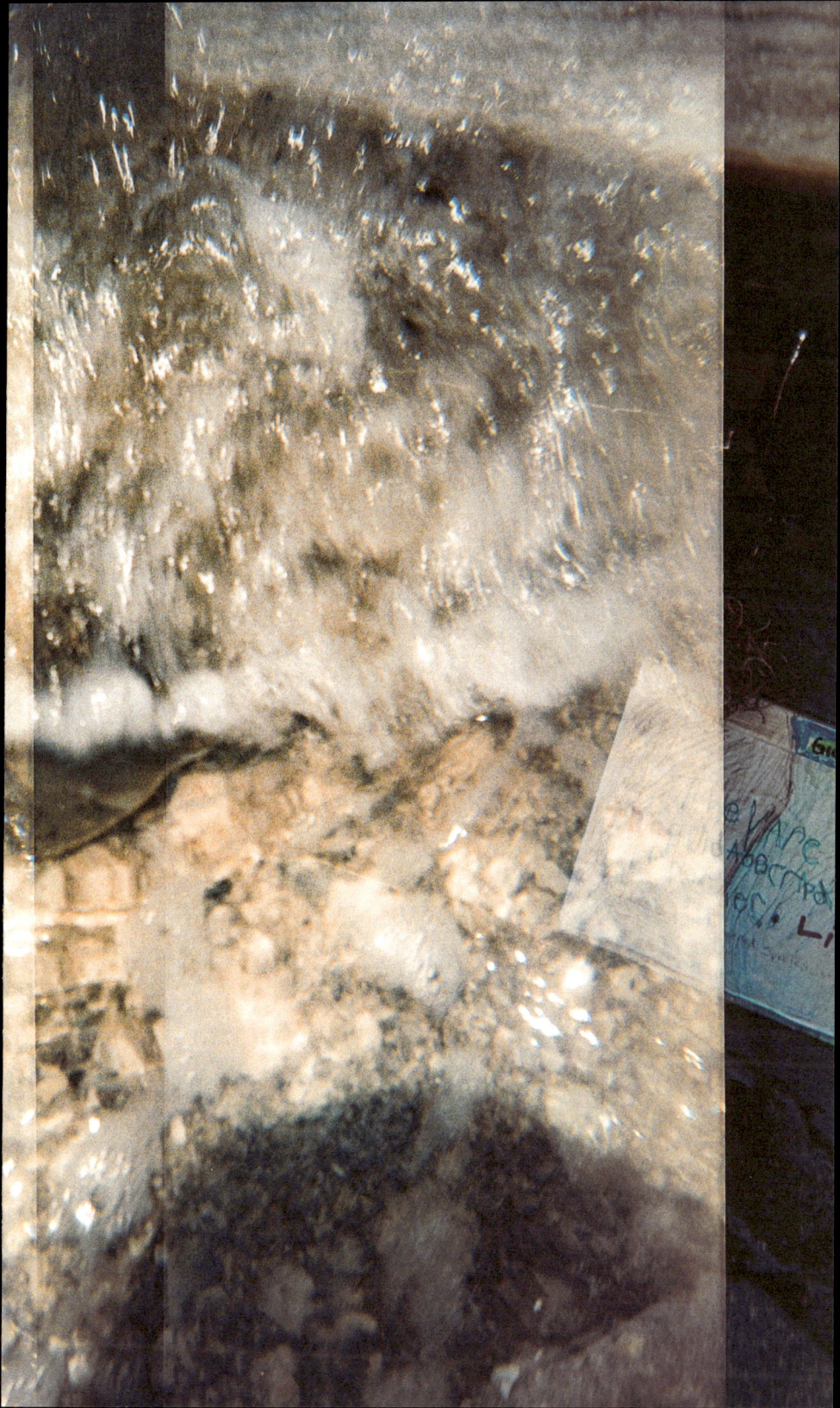

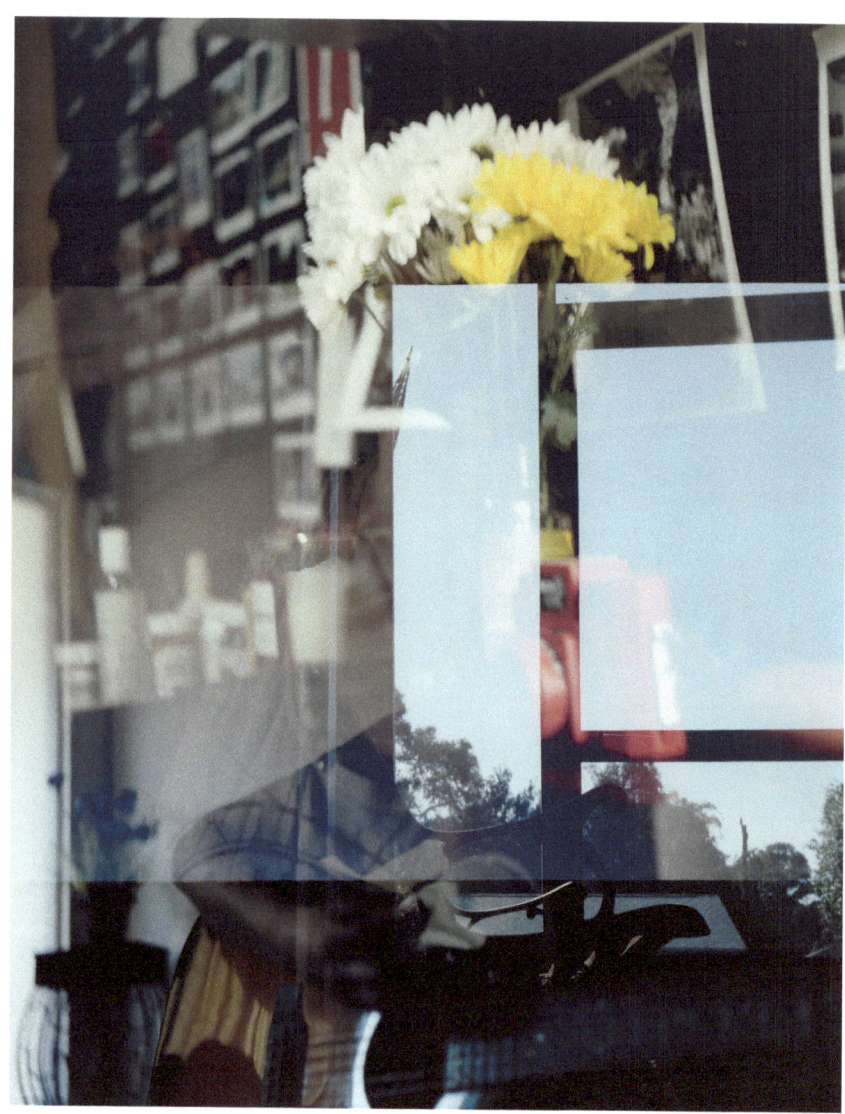

Complacent ingestion,

careless expulsion.

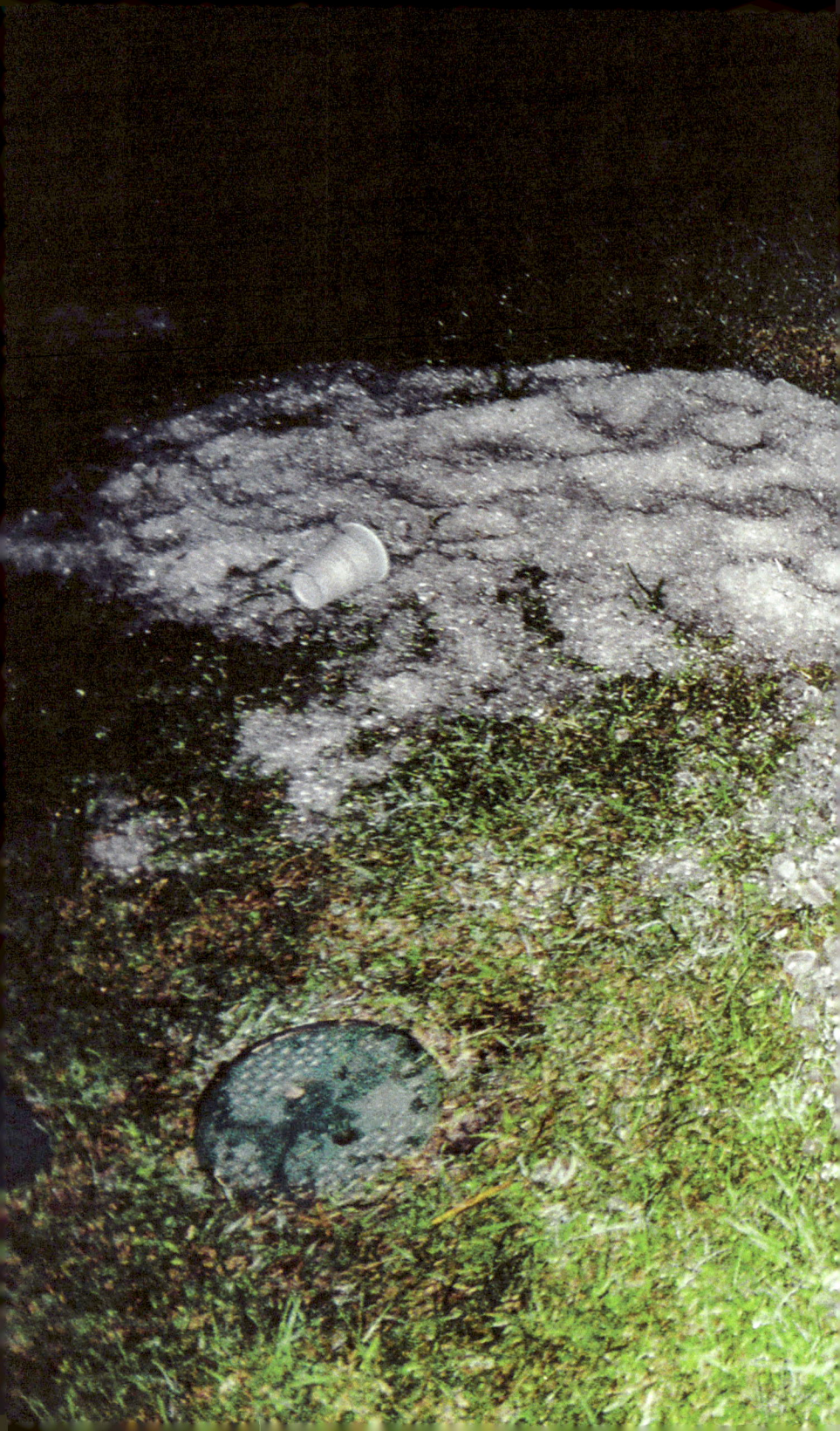

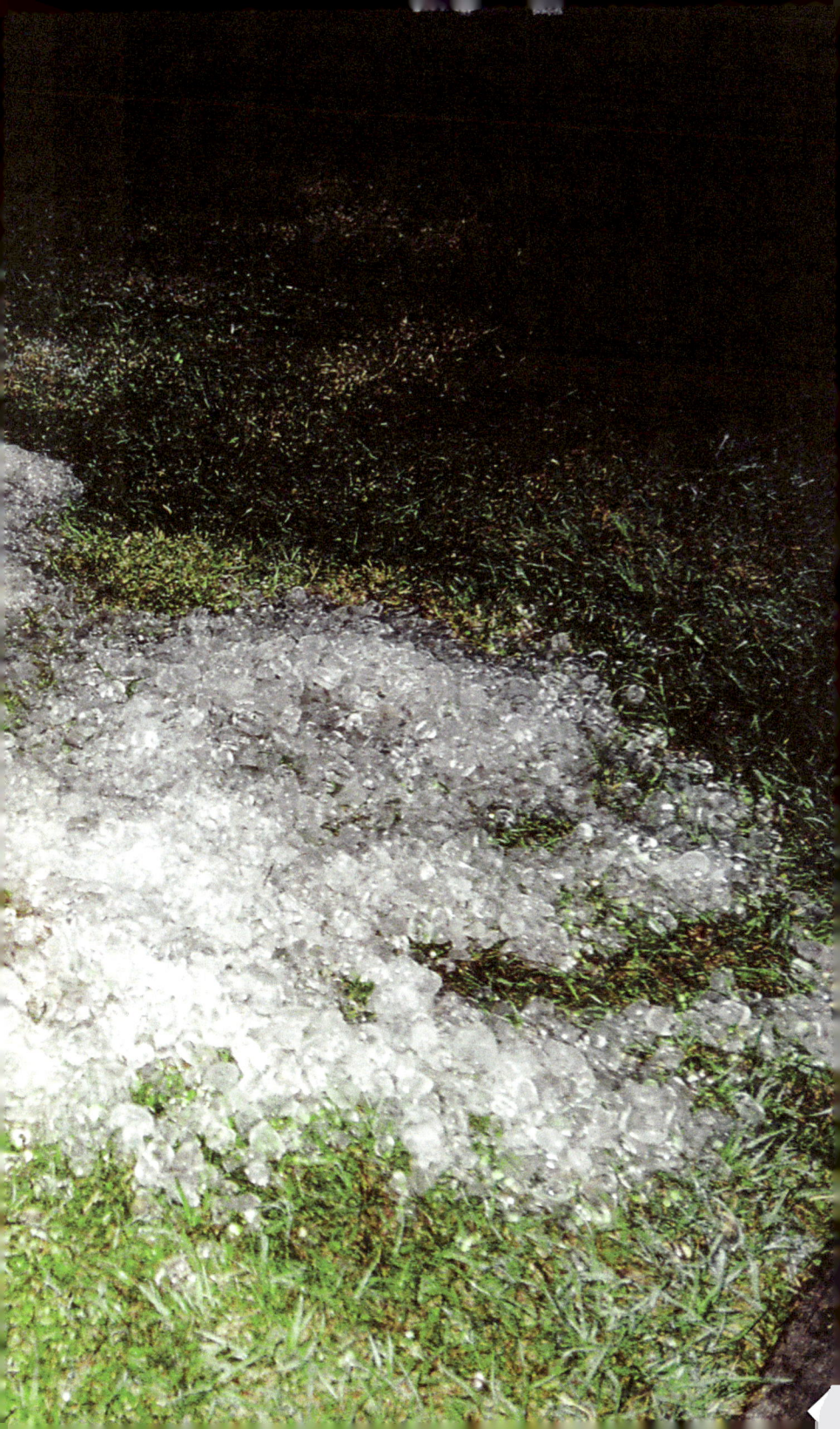

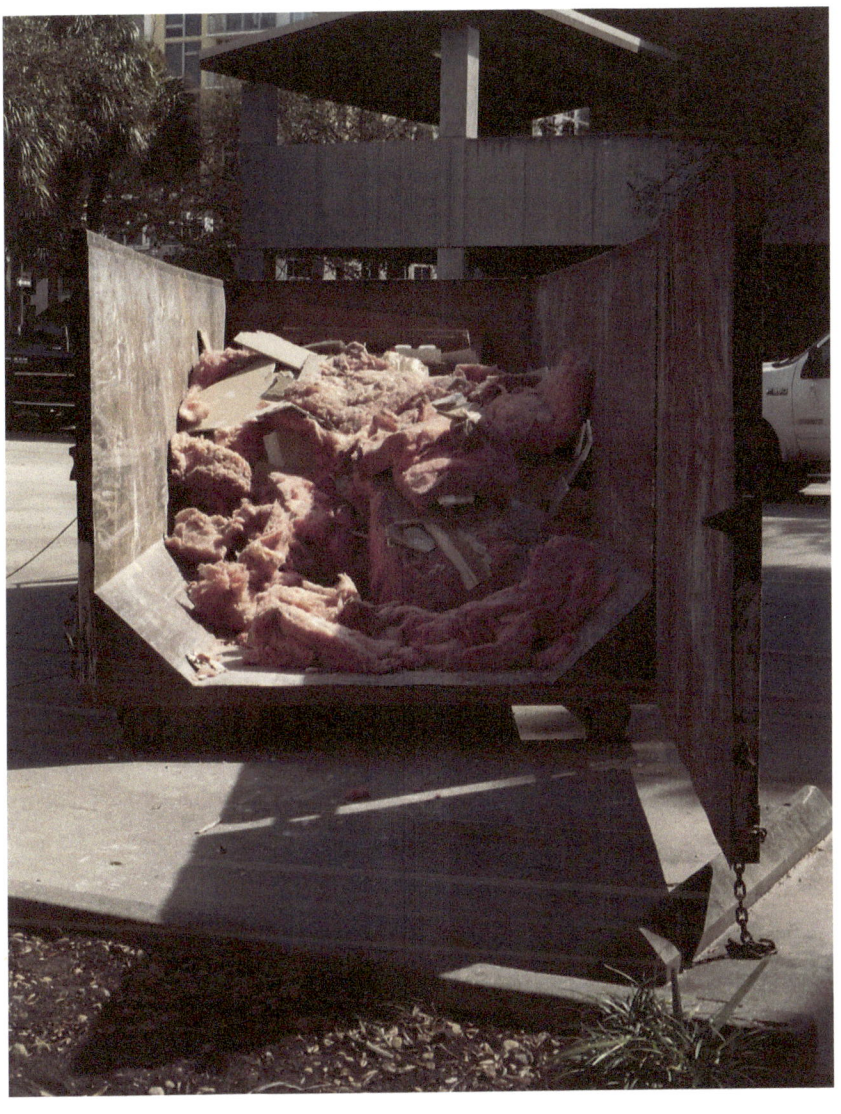

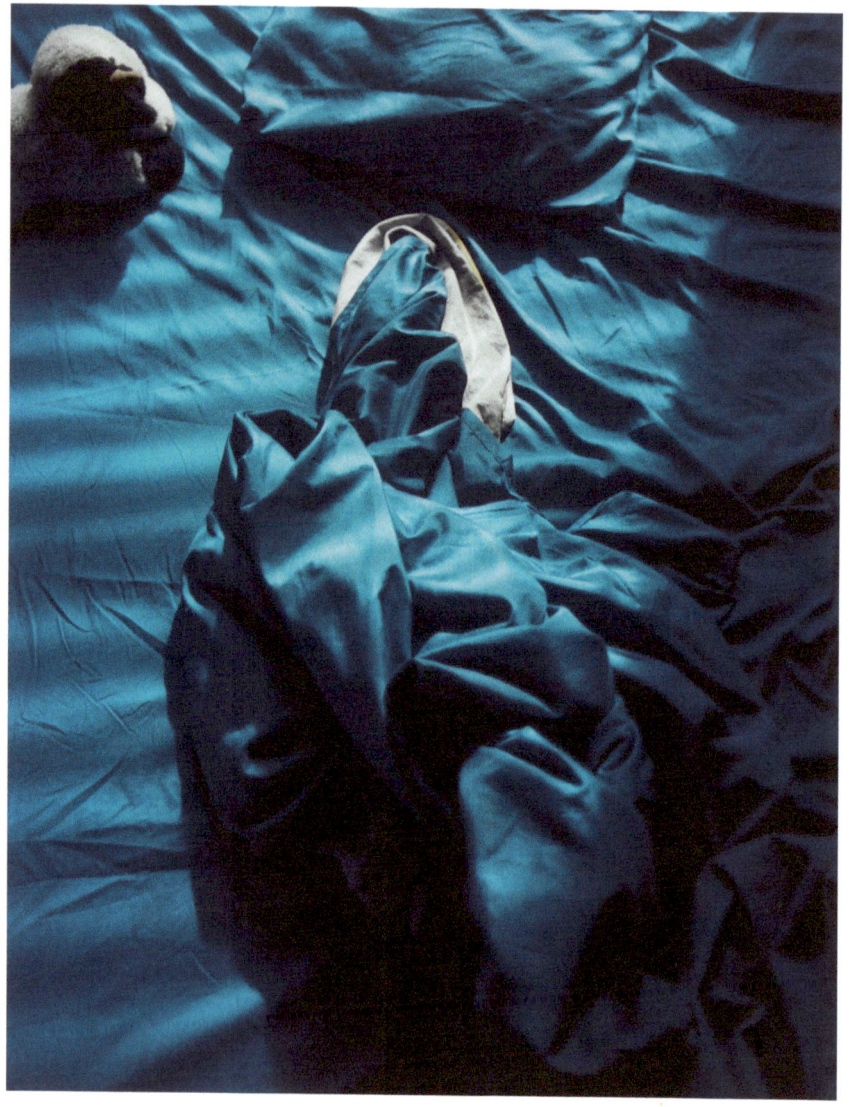

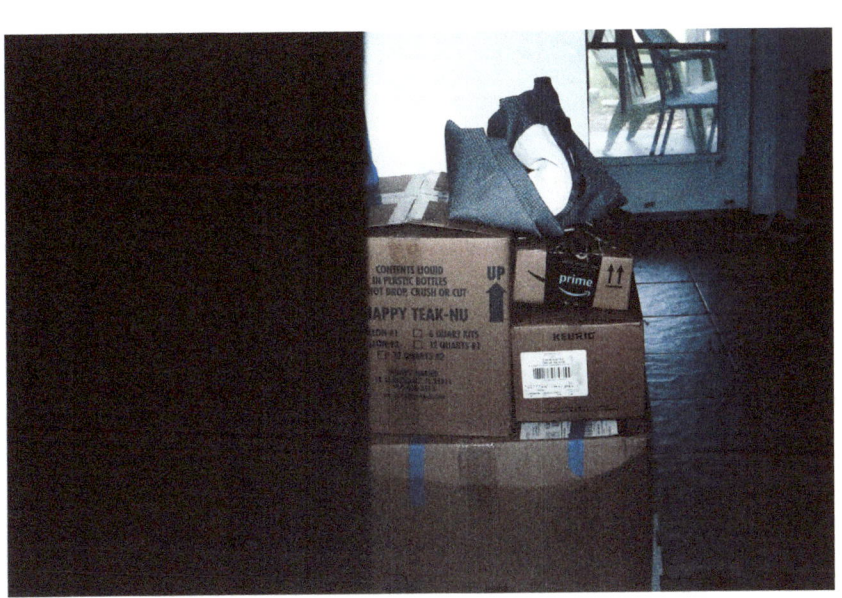

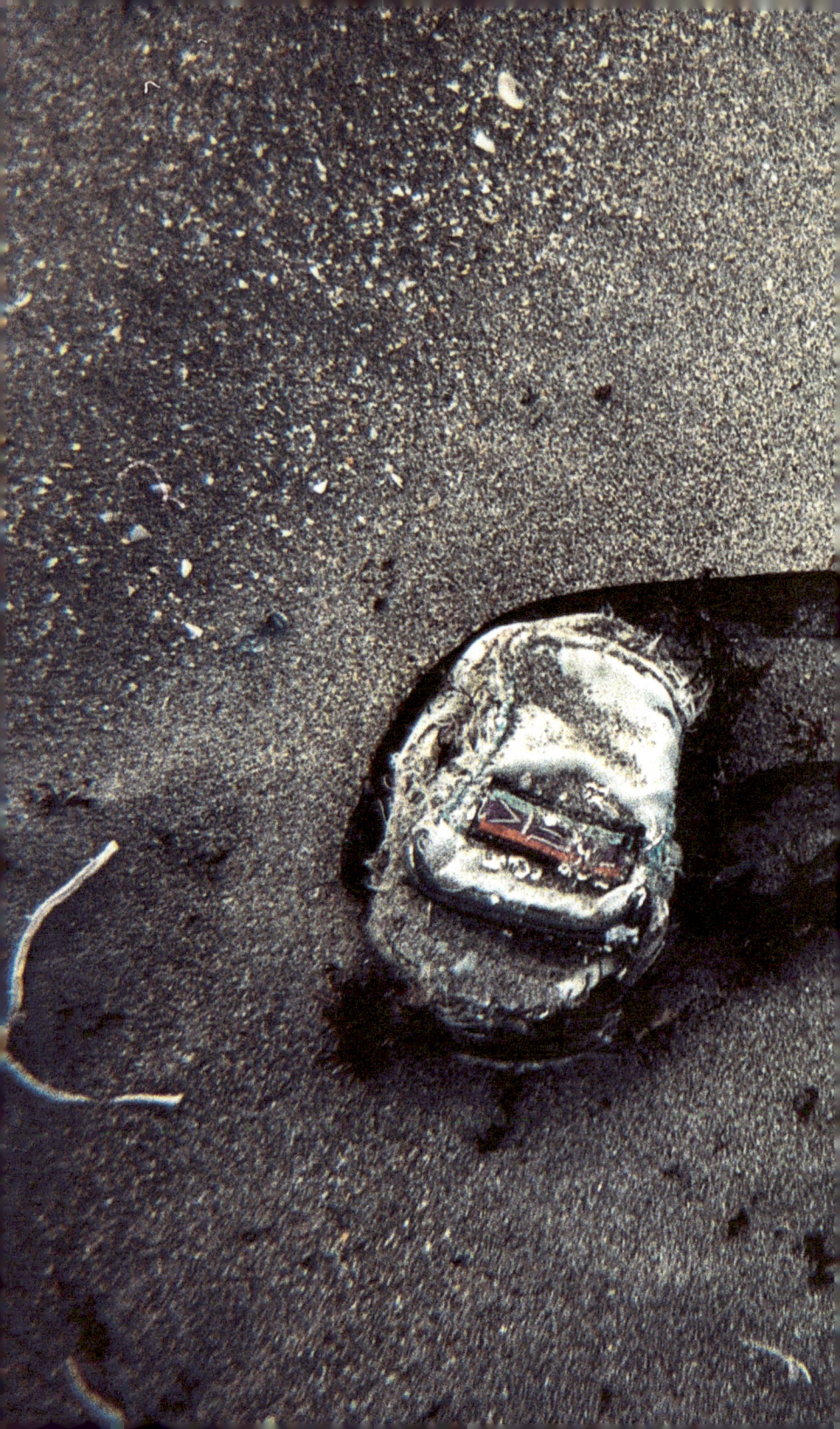

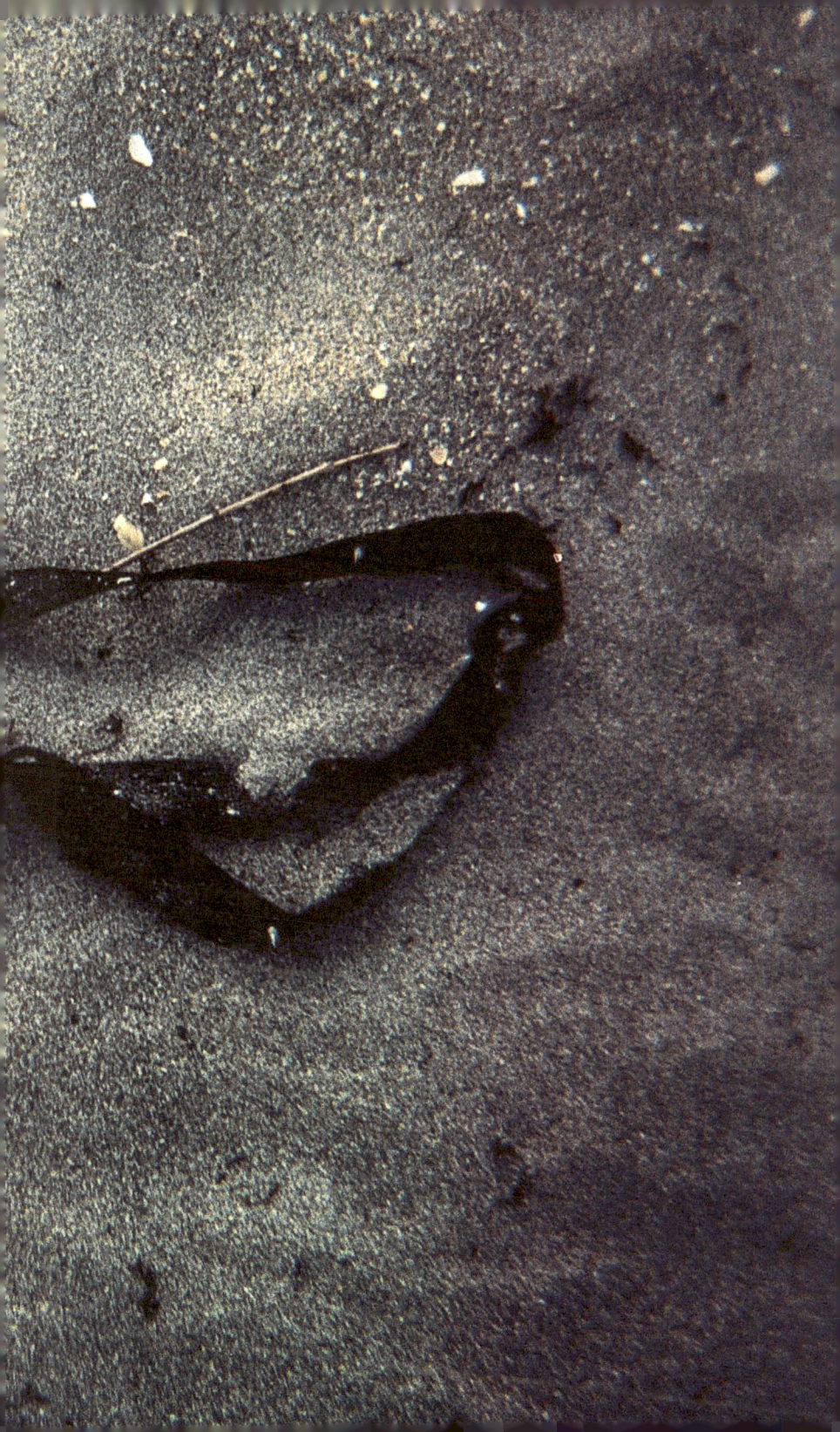

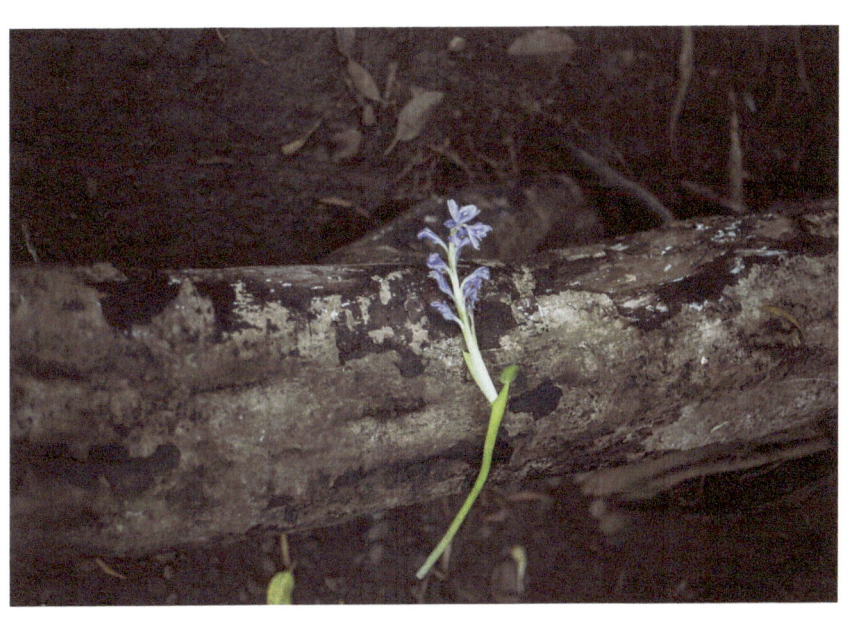

That which remains

after sudden annihilation.

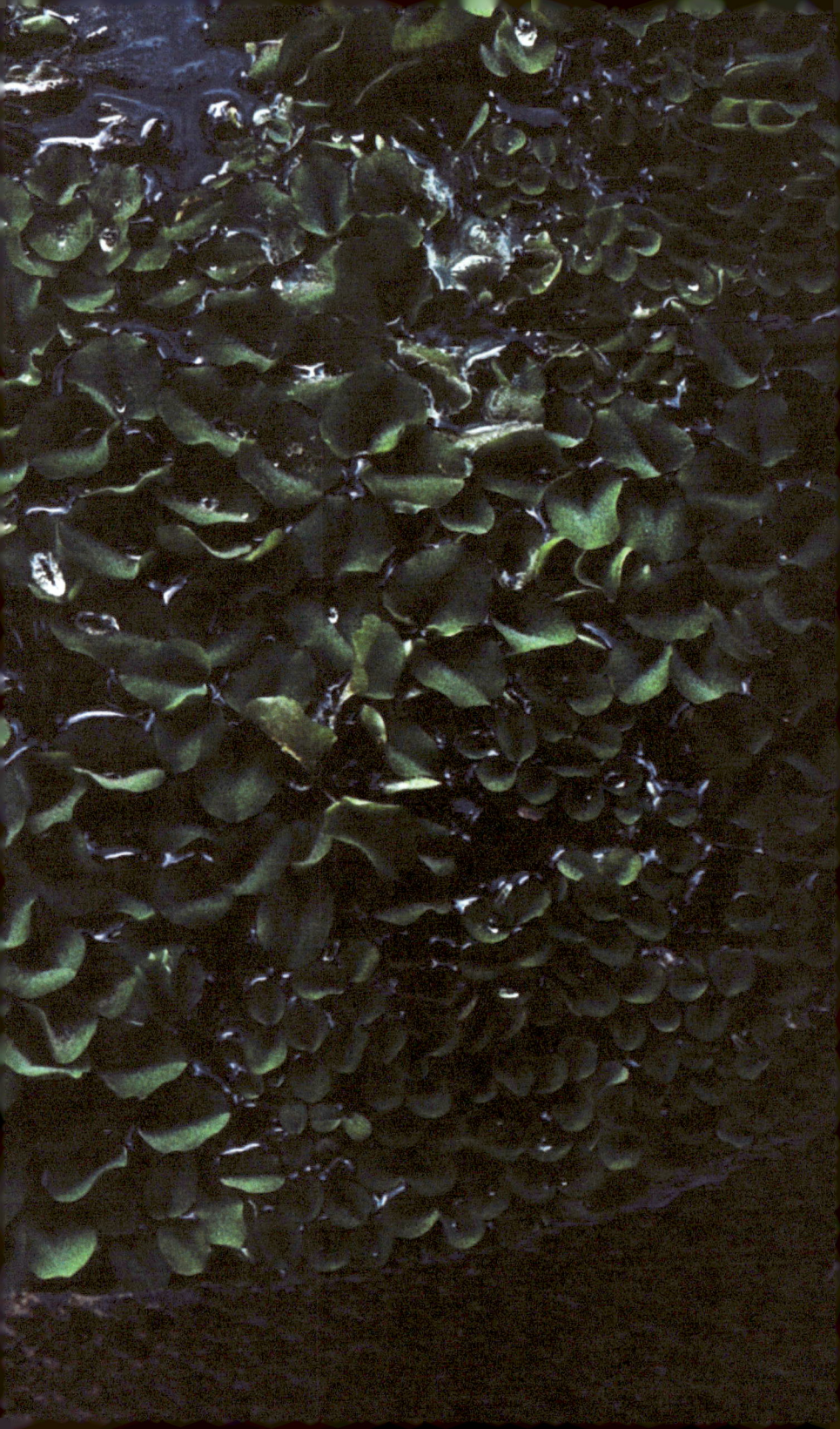

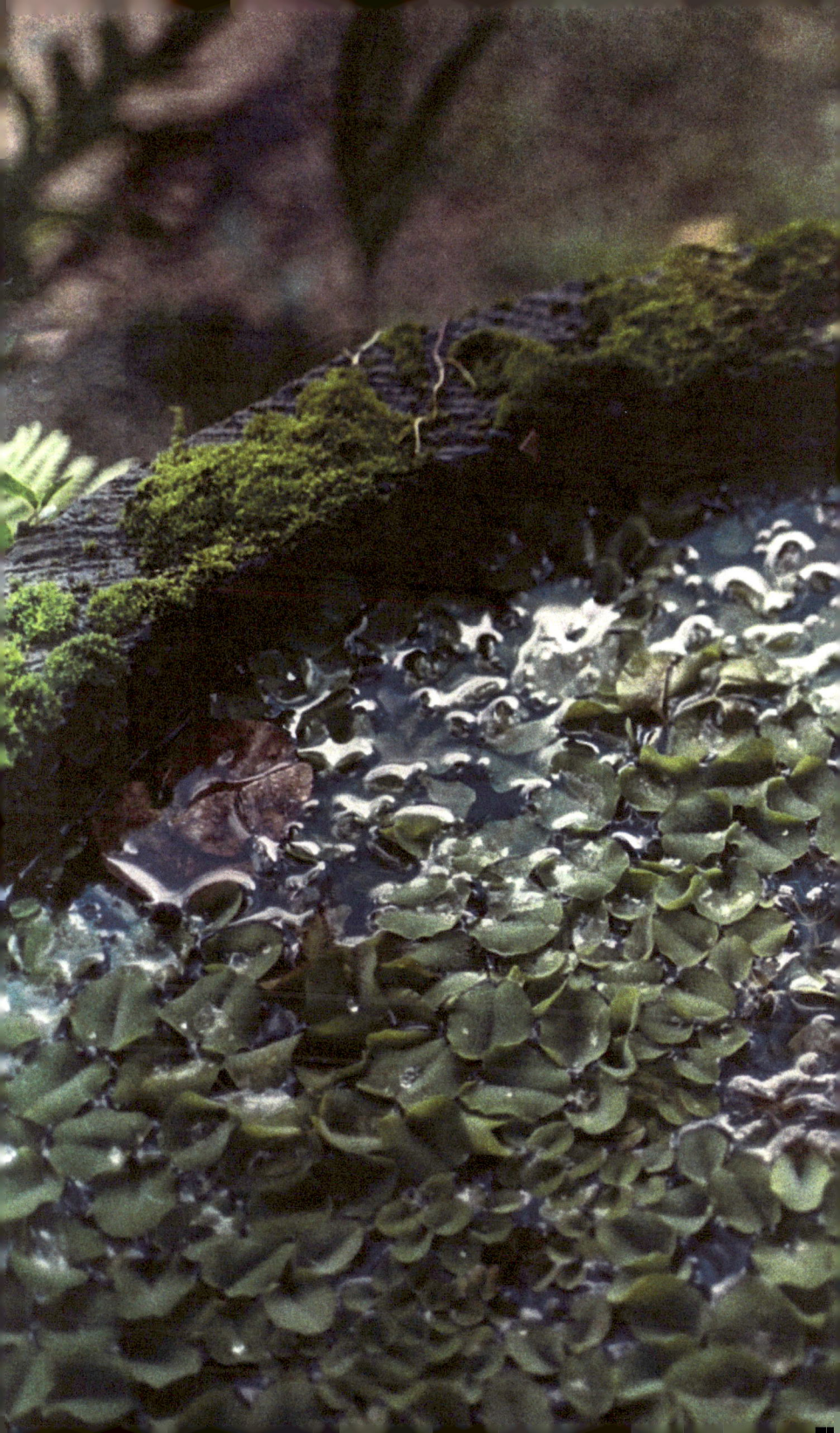

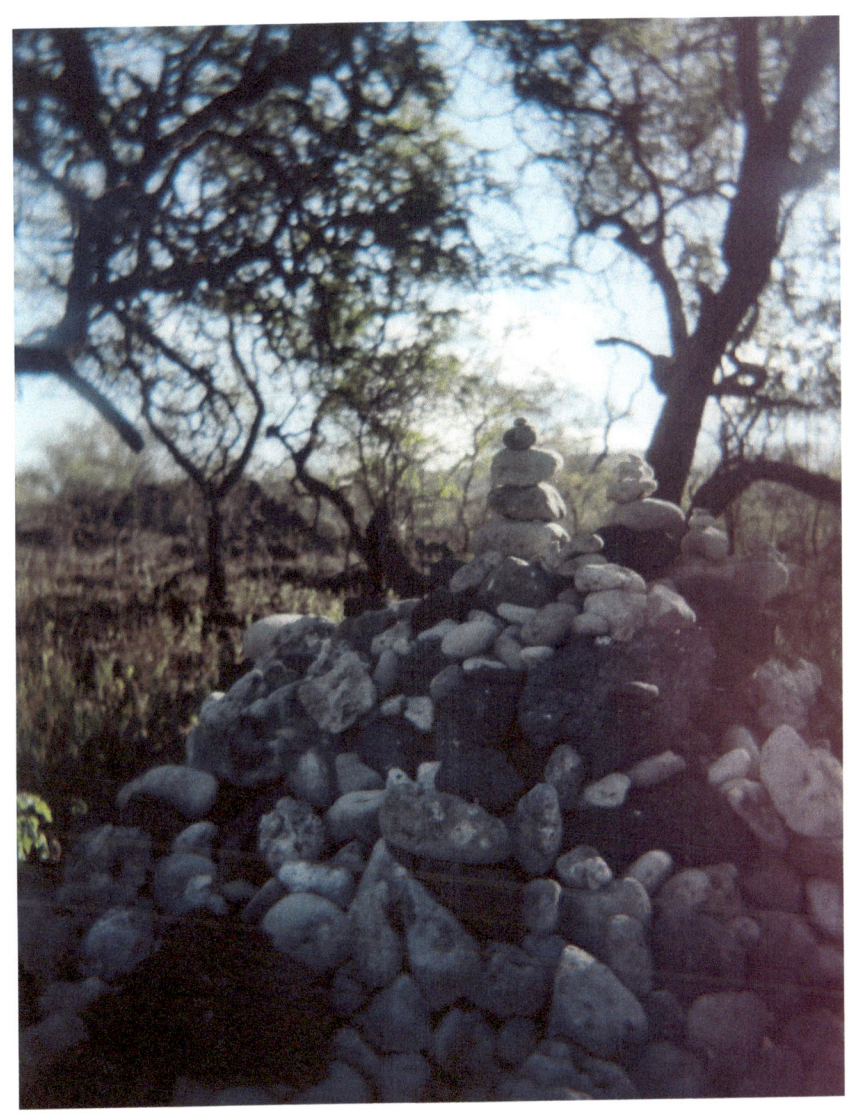

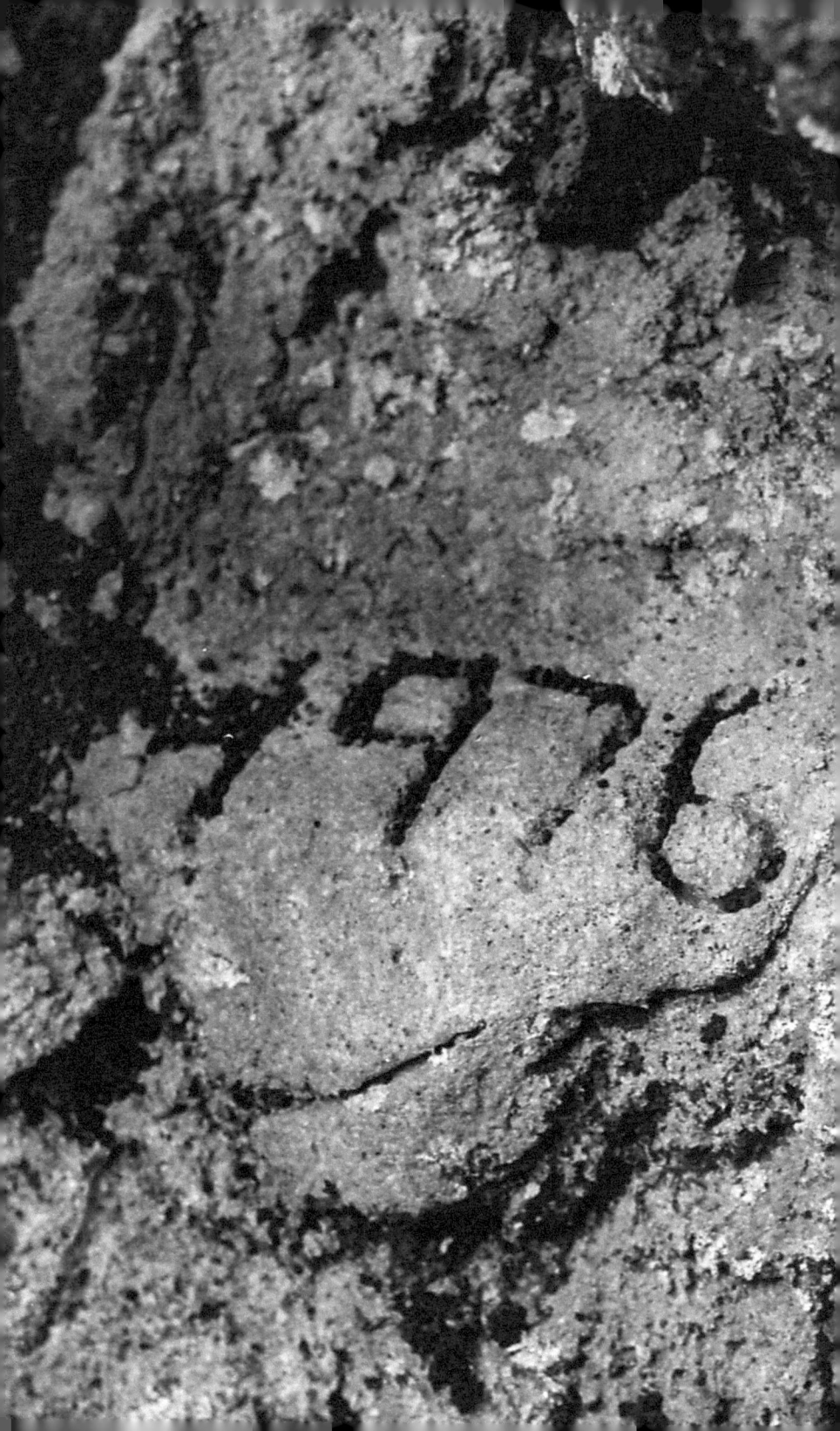

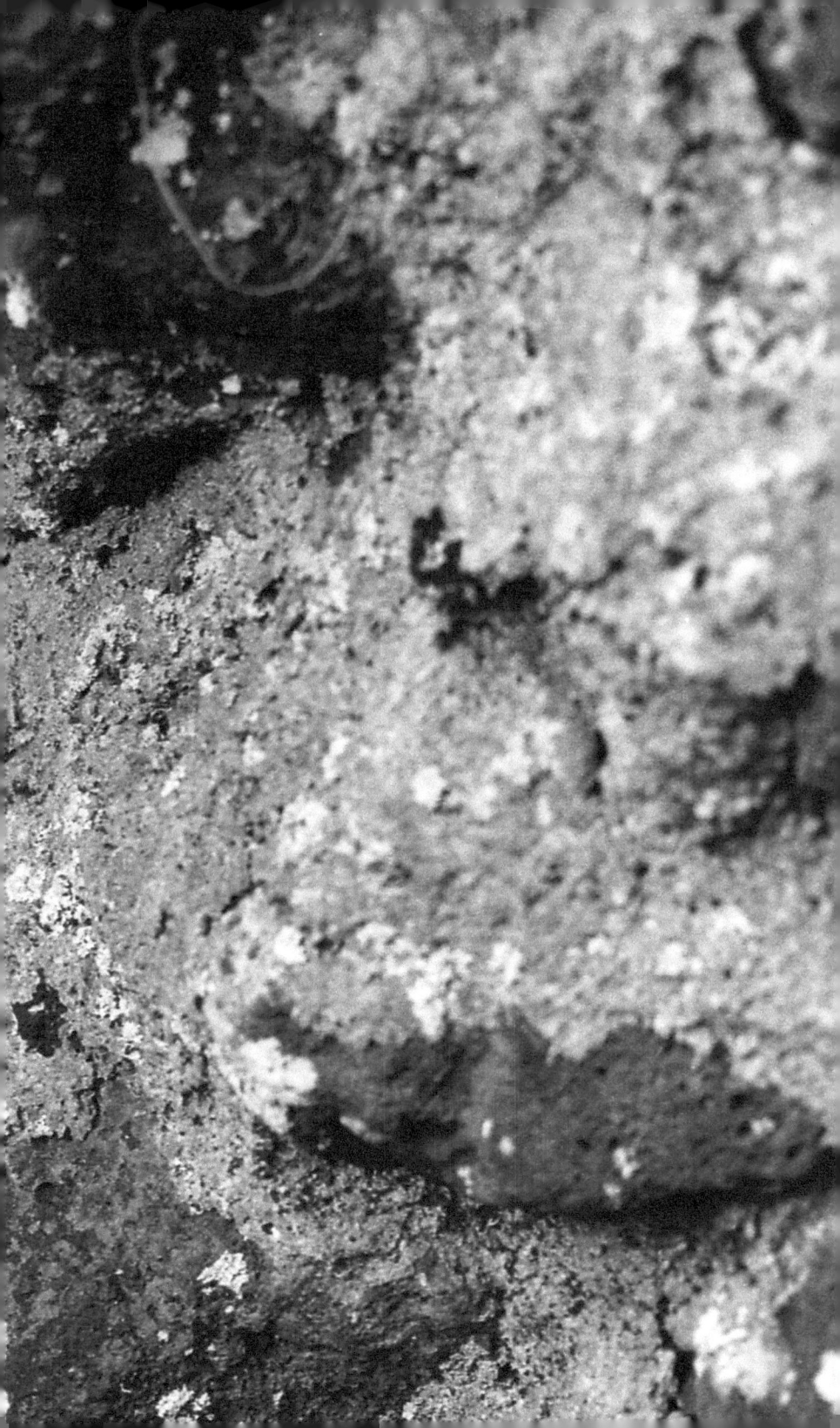

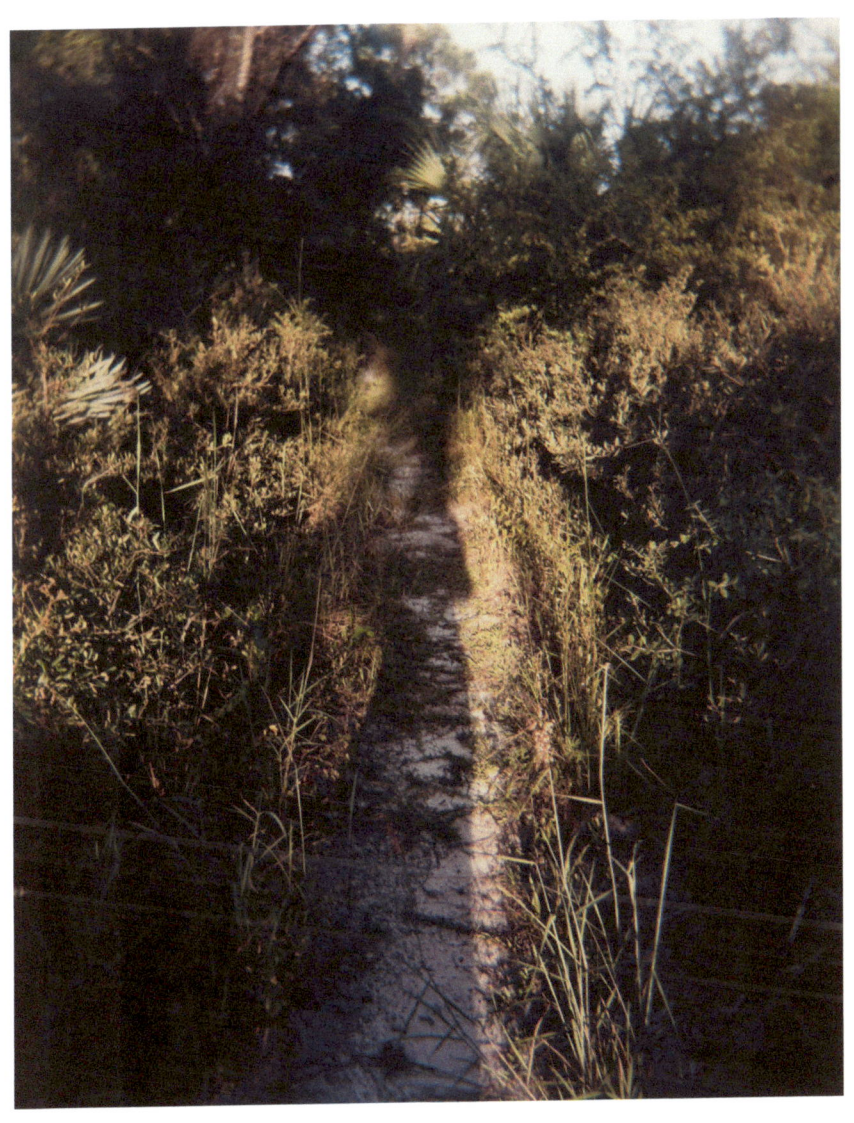

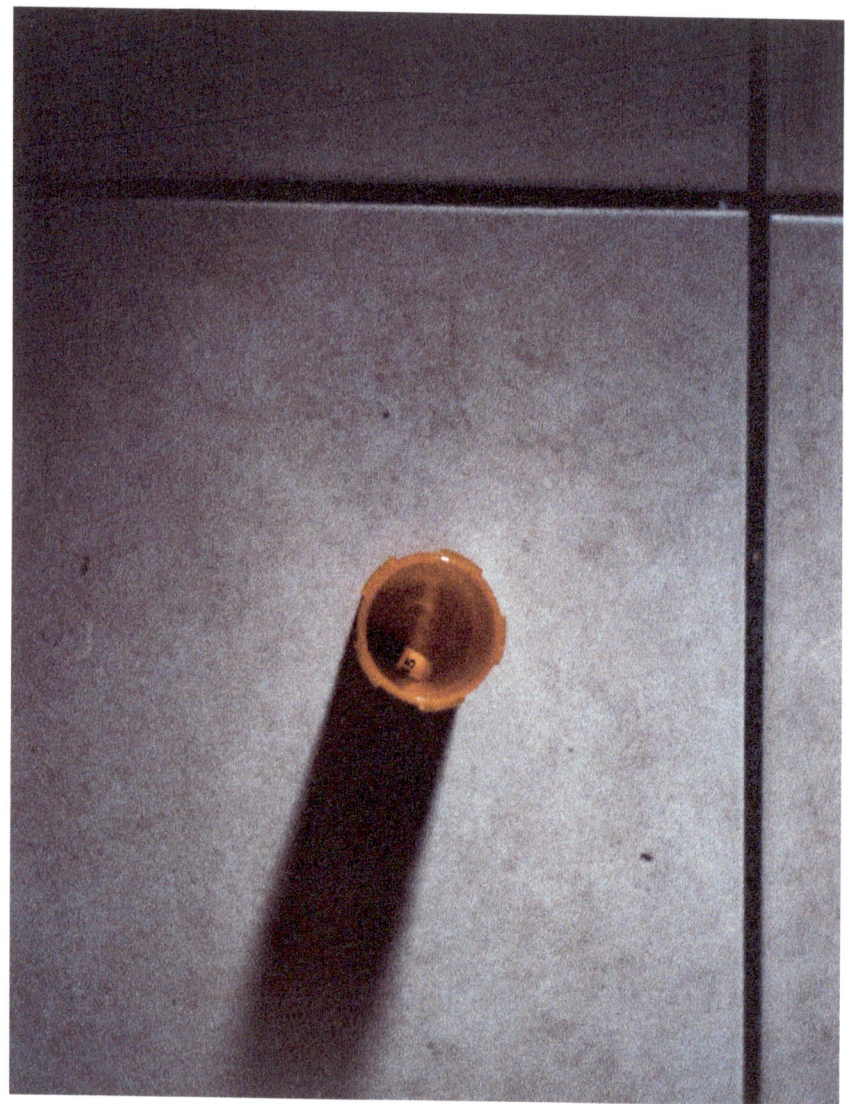

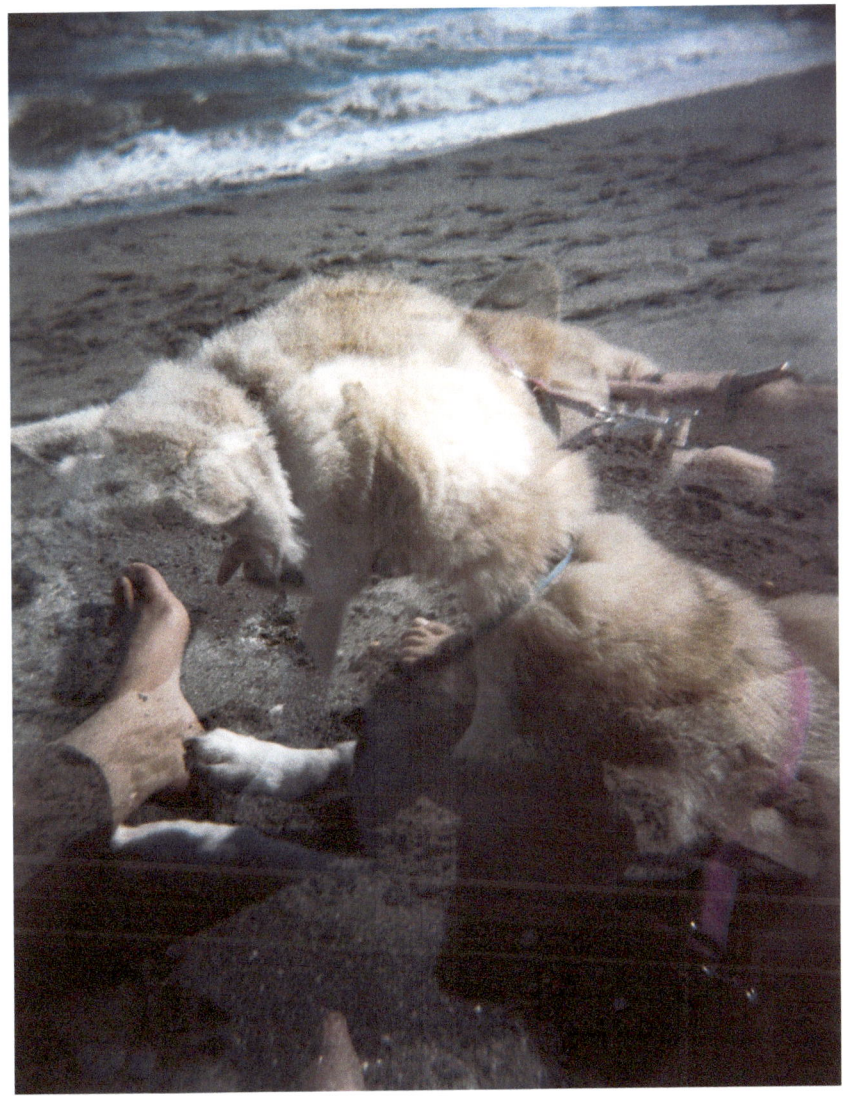

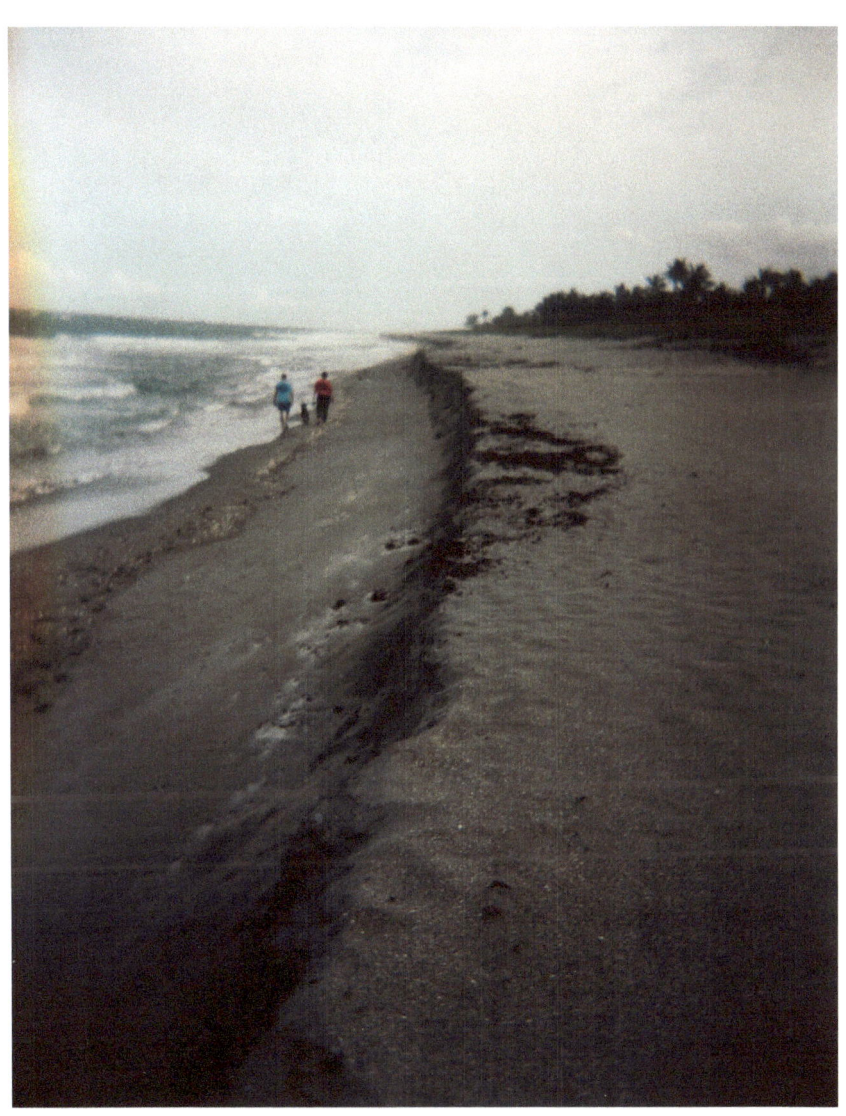

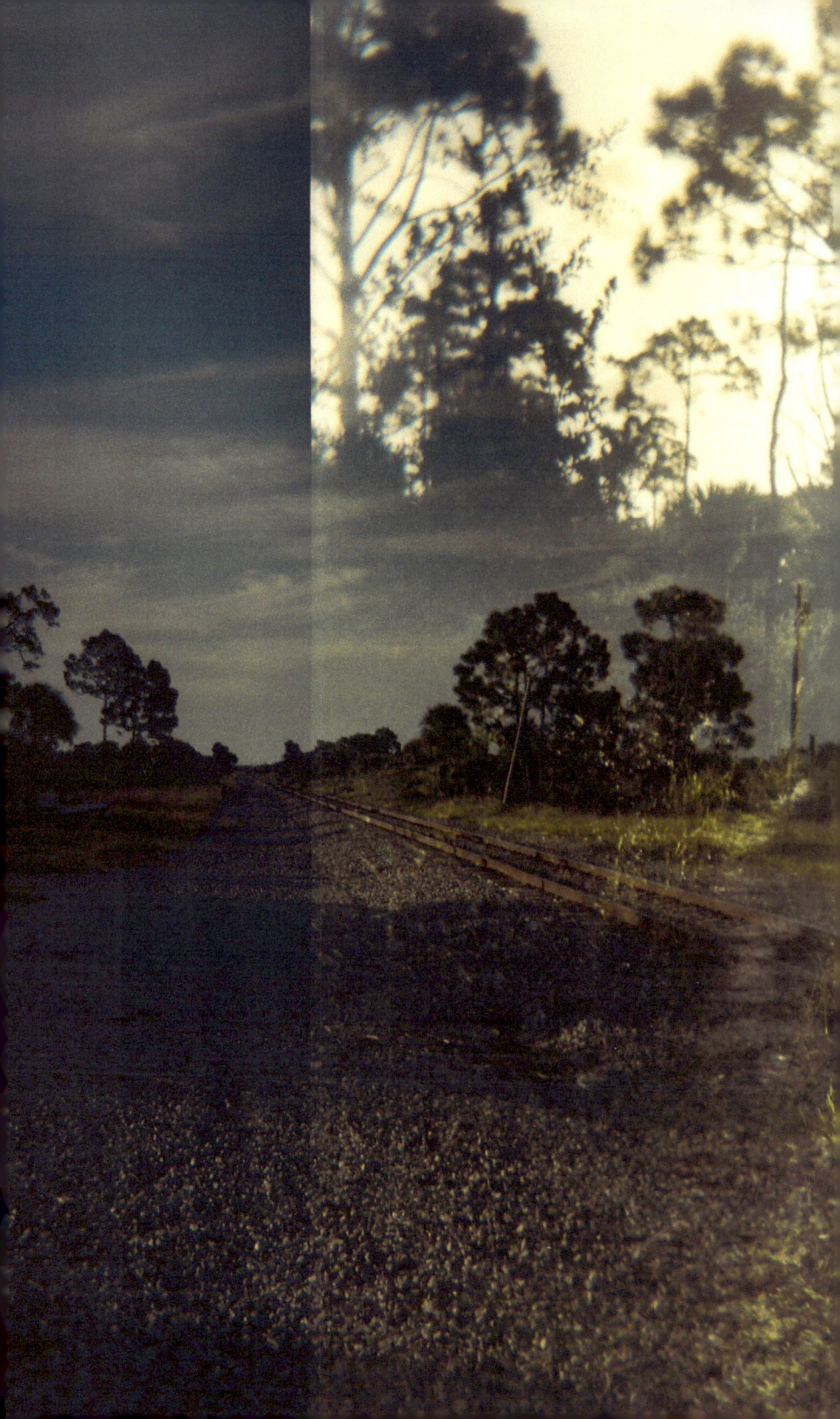

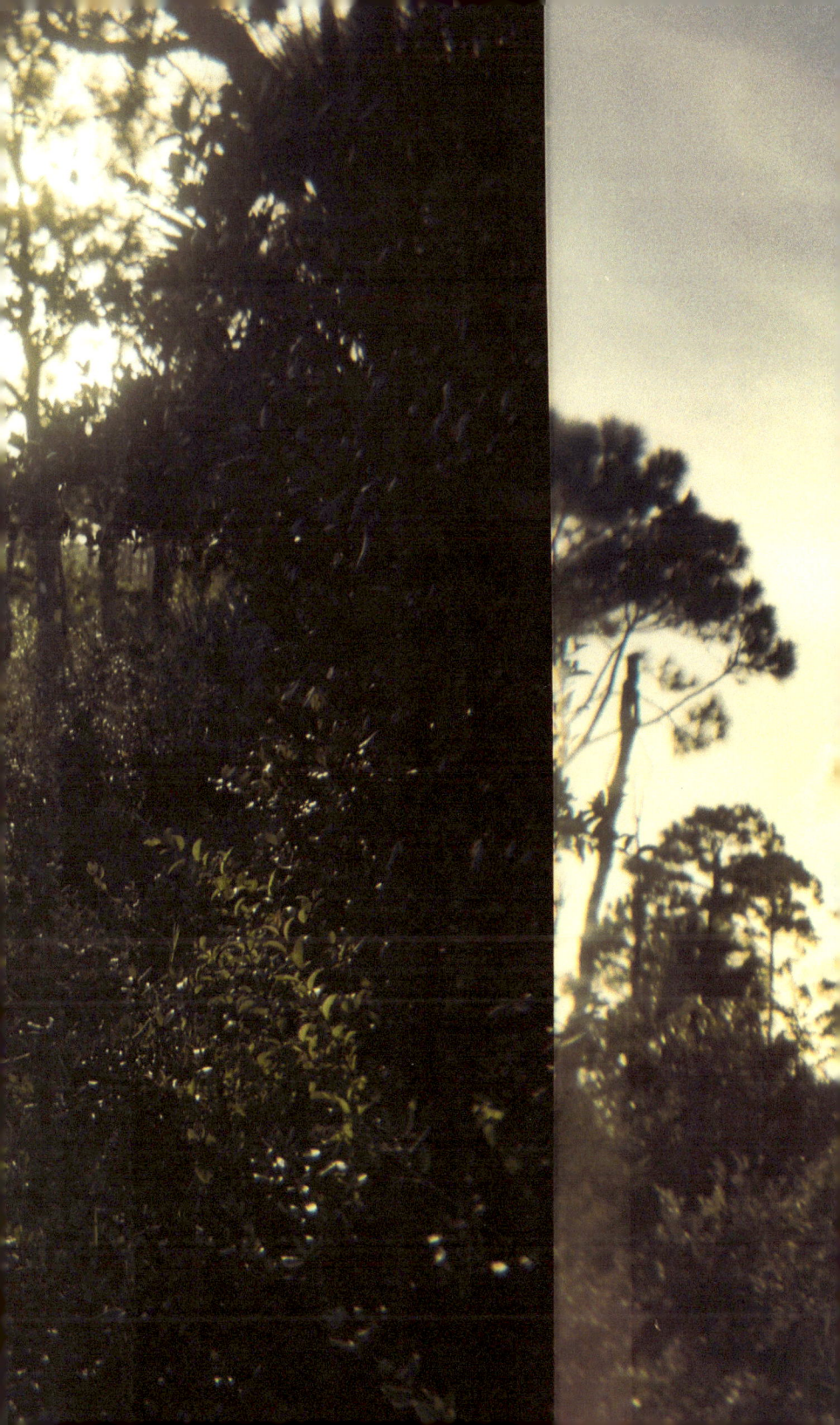

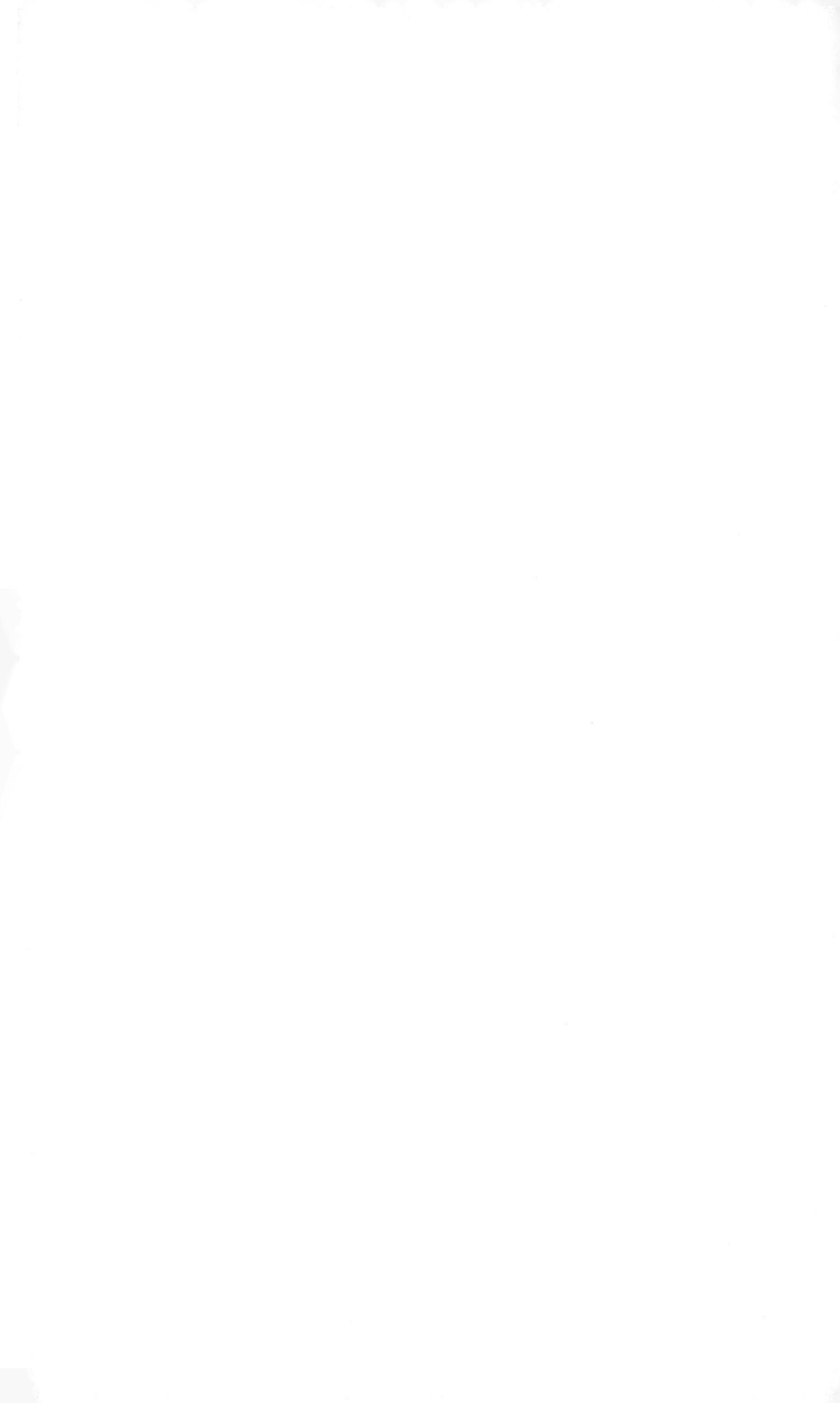

www.ingramcontent.com/pod-product-compliance
Lightning Source LLC
Chambersburg PA
CBHW040330220526
45473CB00009B/2632